Animal Illustrations

TO PAINT OR COLOR

Ruth Soffer

DOVER PUBLICATIONS, INC.
Mineola, New York

Note

In the dense jungles of India lives the tiger, a giant cat that is one of the fiercest predators on earth. Zebras, wild members of the horse family, make their home on the baking savannahs of Africa. Endangered giant pandas are found in the dense bamboo forests of China, while large and gentle manatees, marine mammals, swim in the warm waters of the tropics. Over millions of years, animals have adapted to occupy environmental niches on every continent, including Antarctica. Now this coloring book lets you bring twenty-three different animal species to vibrant life. With crayons, colored pens, pencils, or paints, you can color each animal in its native habitat. Moreover, the drawings are specially printed with light gray lines that virtually disappear with the addition of colors for a polished, professional look. In addition, the pages are perforated so you can remove them from the book when you're finished, and mount them on a wall where you can admire them every day.

Bibliographical Note

Animal Illustrations to Paint or Color is a new work, first published by Dover Publications, Inc., in 2007.

International Standard Book Number
ISBN-13: 978-0-486-45696-6
ISBN-10: 0-486-45696-X

Manufactured in the United States by RR Donnelley
45696X05 2015
www.doverpublications.com